THE SCROLL *of* POSSIBILITIES

Overcoming The Struggles of Life

A Book By

Rev'd Prof. Deborah OkikiJesu JP, PhD, ThD.

The Scroll of Possibilities: Overcoming the Struggles of Life

ISBN: 978-9-3258-8613-1

Publish by:
Emphaloz Publishing House
www.emphaloz.com
publish@emphaloz.com

Printed and Available Globally

This book is dedicated to God Almighty the author and finisher of our faith

ACKNOWLEDGEMENT

From the Heart

I want to seize this opportunity to express my deepest appreciation to my Lord and Saviour, Jesus Christ, the Author and Finisher of my faith, for making this dream a reality. Without His grace, permission, and unwavering love, especially in my imperfections, this work would not have been possible. Glory Hallelujah.

From the bottom of my heart, I extend my heartfelt gratitude to my co-authors, who, despite their busy schedules, devoted their time and wisdom to help bring this book to life. In no particular order:

- Pastor Babatunde Soniregun (Canada)
- Pastor Esther Aramide Olujimi (UK)
- Prophetess Mercy Magbagbeola (UK)
- Pastor Samuel Terry (Canada)
- Rabbi Sup. Evang. Joel Adegoke (UK)
- Pastor Honey Emmanuel-Molokwu (Nigeria/UK)

I pray for my co-writers that God will continually grant you wisdom, clarity, and grace. May the works of your hands be established, your voices strengthened, and your impact multiplied. May this book speak life through us all, in Jesus' name. Amen.

My sincere thanks also go to Prof. Pastor Dr. David Soile and M/C Similolu Ojelade (Life Patron and Matron of El Bethel Ministries). I truly cannot thank you enough for believing in this vision.

Pastor Dr.Tayo Ogunmefun, Prophet Oluwafemi Ajayi, Rev'd Anthony Akindutire, VSE Samuel Akinyemi, VSE Olalekan Kusoro, Rev. Mother Pro. Abosede Otusile, I deeply appreciate your contributions, wisdom, and guidance. VSE Babatunde Soile (VOJC), Rev'd Pa, David Adeoye, words are not enough, thank you all for everything.

To my lovely mother, Lady Evangelist E. A. Terry (Abiyamo Tooto), thank you for your constant prayers and love. Sufficient grace to you, Maami.

In loving memory of my father, the late Pastor Engr. J. B. Terry, we remain forever grateful for the wisdom you imparted to us, your children. How I wish you were still here. Continue to rest in glory, Dad.

Evangelist Kunle Olowokere and family, you are truly wonderful. The Celestial Honours Award, VSE. Ebenezer, thanks for your support.

Pastor Samuel Terry, GoWorld Ministries, thank you for believing in this vision. Lady Evang Thelma Suma-Keita, thanks for all that you do.

To the entire Trustees of El Bethel Prayer Tabernacle, friends and family both at home and abroad, I deeply appreciate your steadfast support. I do not take it for granted.

To my beautiful children, my siblings, and my in-laws, wherever you may be in the world, I love you dearly.

If I had my way, I would mention as many names as possible in this book, but space would not permit it. Nevertheless, I sincerely appreciate everyone whom God has used in my life, in one way or another, even if I did not mention their names; God knows them. I pray that on your journey through life, you will never be short of good helpers, in Jesus' name. Amen.

I remain yours in His Service,
Rev'd Prof Deborah OkikiJesu JP ThD.

Table of Contents

FOREWORD

Prof. Okikijesu

Matthew 21:42 *says, have you never read in the Scriptures: 'The stone the builders rejected has become the Cornerstone; this is the Lord's doing, and it is marvellous in our eyes.'" Which means, rejection doesn't cancel God's purpose. What others dismiss, God can elevate. Your outcome is shaped by God, not by critics.*

I am deeply grateful to everyone whom God has used, and continues to use, to support me and this ministry on my life's journey. I am just as thankful for those who said "no" and for those who tried to discourage or undermine this dream. They, too, played a role in shaping this testimony of growth and victory. Over the years, I have realised that two of the greatest barriers to change are fear and procrastination. Success often appears impossible until it is finally achieved. It is important to understand that the most powerful gift you possess is yourself, your voice, your mind, your story, and your vision. A moment of disappointment does not define your destiny. My vision in life is not merely to survive, but to thrive, and to do so with purpose, confidence, and grace. I am reminded of a former colleague who often said, half in jest yet full of truth, that "death is not the greatest loss in life; the greatest loss is the vision that dies within us while we are still alive."

INTRODUCTION

Prof. Okikijesu

No matter where you are on your life's journey, you will soon discover that the road is not always easy. Though we all desire a life free of troubles, reality often unfolds differently. Along the way, doubt, fear, and moments of weakened confidence will present themselves. Yet God's promise in Jeremiah 29:11 *has been a sustaining light for me through my darkest seasons: "For I know the thoughts that I think toward you, saith the Lord, thoughts of peace and not of evil, to give you an expected end."*

Throughout life, you will inevitably encounter three distinct types of people. The first are those who sincerely desire your advancement and will go to great lengths to support you. These are the encouragers, people who see potential where others see flaws.

The second group comprises those who appear interested in your journey but ultimately contribute nothing meaningful. They linger on the sidelines, offering neither help nor genuine concern; they drain your energy rather than add value.

The third group includes those who simply do not care about your growth. To them, your efforts, progress, and success mean little. They criticise easily, find fault in everything, and remain unmoved regardless of your achievements.

Though these groups differ greatly, each plays a defining role in shaping who we become. We cannot avoid meeting them; they are woven into the fabric of our development. You may ask, *"Why must I encounter all these types of people?"* The answer is simple: each one forms part of the structure of your growth, the foundation, the middle, and the finishing layer of your life's building.

This book reveals how to recognise these influences, rise above their challenges, and embrace the lessons they bring. This book unfolds a scroll of possibilities, revealing how God uses every encounter, whether joyful or painful, to shape you for your purpose and your expected end.

THE TEST OF TIME

Prof. Okikijesu

In life, no one hits you harder than life itself. It doesn't matter how hard you hit back; it will always be down to how much you can take.

All my life, I was terrified of failure; unfortunately, life is not built like that. Many times, you have to fail to succeed, but not many people can handle the negative effect or the aftermath of being tagged a failure by society. Sometimes, the shame of being a disappointment in one's life journey may lead to self-rejection and negative thoughts. If one is not careful, it can cripple someone and lock that person in mental slavery. This experience takes me back to a snippet of my life. There is a saying that says, 'You cannot take people there unless you have been there. And that is why I feel qualified to share my personal journey.

I had a good childhood and came from a loving, Christian home. My parents were strict disciplinarians yet deeply loving at all times. I could not have asked for more. As the firstborn in a family of six, I found myself in a position where my five younger siblings looked up to me as a role model. To me, it was a huge responsibility. However, growing up in such a nurturing environment and transitioning through my teenage years into a responsible adult did not fully prepared me for the cruelty of the world beyond our home. Life betrayed me, and the pain was overwhelming. Instead of sharing what I was going through with my family, I saw myself as a total failure. Trusting people became increasingly difficult; I completely lost myself. At the time, I believed no one could help me; I longed for an easy way out because I was simply too tired to carry on. I told myself I had already failed and that there was no way forward. I worried about what people would say, that my despair had driven me to consider taking my own life. But little did I know what God had in store for my future. Every attempt proved abortive, and though the struggle continued, my ordeal was far from over.

I let my situation at the time get the better of me, and it masked how God released me from the claws of death when I was giving birth to my Son at the time. A labour that took four agonising days and later resulted in a gruesome emergency caesarean section! And how God brought me back to life after the Doctors said I may not make it back due to complications at childbirth, and even if I did, I may not be able to have another child? I was very ungrateful. I was still asking God, why me? Long story short, God has been faithful. I lived to tell the story and testify to His faithfulness. Please understand, my dear readers, that my intention is not to gain sympathy, but I want my readers to understand that life's challenges can feel overwhelming and discouraging, and at times, they can shake you when you're going through difficult seasons. It is easy to get blinded by people's negative perceptions of you and completely forget about the bigger picture. Believe me, I have been there, so I know.

Arguing with people when they put you down or discourage you with a sour word that you can't do something right or that you are a failure, I don't think it's worth it. Until you prove them wrong and show them what you are worth, you will not be free from mental slavery. Thank God for my redemption.

Moreover, the unsettling side of life can leave you feeling downtrodden, especially if you fall into the category of the ambitious ones like me. It could be very challenging, not able to climb your ladder of success to its pinnacle, or when you constantly experience devastating rejection, most especially from the people that you thought did love you and would jump through the hoops for you, then it dawned on you that it is a big mistake leaning on the understanding of man all along.

Psalm 146, verse 3-5 *says; Do not put your trust in princes, in human beings, who cannot save. When their spirit departs, they return to the ground; on that very day, their plans come to nothing. Blessed are those whose help is the God of Jacob; whose hope is in the LORD their God.*

In the journey of life, as we climb the ladder of success, we need to know that there is going to be a slippery side of the ladder, whether we like it or not. But our reaction, approach, and determination to keep going and succeed matter a lot. If you are reading this book or just peeping through, you need to know that it's not over until God says it's over. This book is filled with the knowledge of His will, and I pray that the book will serve as a reminder that God loves you, irrespective of your horrible past or present.

What Are Your Stressors?

- Is it the death of a loved one?
- Loss of a job?
- Chronic illness or life-changing injury?
- Divorce?
- Increase in financial obligation?
- Waiting for a fruit of the womb?
- Emotional issues leading to depression, anxiety, guilt, or low self-esteem, and so many more.

Overall, ineffectively managed stress usually takes a toll on the body when prolonged. But inner peace of mind refers to a deliberate state of psychological or spiritual calm despite the potential presence of stressors.

Gone are the days when I was completely engulfed by the turmoil of life. There was a season when the wilderness of my circumstances surrounded me so intensely that I could no longer see a path forward. The weight of it all felt unbearable, and in my darkest moments, I convinced myself that ending everything was the only solution. But I was wrong.

What I once believed was the end was, in truth, the turning point. The very place where I felt the most lost became the ground on which God began to rebuild me. What I thought was my breaking became the beginning of my becoming.

JUMPING THROUGH THE HURDLES OF LIFE

Prof. Okikijesu

Life rarely announces its storms in advance. Challenges do not always come in gentle showers; at times, they descend with the force of a torrential downpour. These seasons can feel unrelenting moments when difficulties gather all at once, testing the limits of our endurance and the depth of our faith.

Yet within these overwhelming periods lie profound opportunities for growth. It is often in the heaviest rains that we discover the strength we did not know we had, the clarity we never imagined possible, and the resilience that carries us forward. Though the storm may be fierce, it does not come to break us, but to shape us into who we are meant to be.

STAYING POSITIVE

Prof. Okikijesu

A colleague asked me some time ago how I have managed to remain positive despite the many hurdles I have faced in life. I smiled and told him this simple truth: *I don't know anyone who has never felt depressed at some point in their journey, but how you rise above those moments depends on you, and on your faith.*

So, how do you stay positive after a series of bumps and bruises along the way?

Staying positive requires *intentional training of the mind*. It involves choosing to look for the good around you, even when life feels overwhelming. When you shift your focus, you'll begin to notice that there is always something, no matter how small, to be grateful for.

Listening to the stories of others also brings perspective. You realise that, although your situation may be challenging, it could have been far worse. And in that awareness, you find strength and hope to keep going. Positivity does not deny reality; it simply refuses to let reality defeat you.

BREAKING OFF FROM YOUR LIMITATIONS

Prof. Okikijesu

Breaking free from personal limitations can be frightening. Without intentional effort, fear can easily give way to procrastination, delaying progress until change feels almost impossible. Yet the truth remains: you cannot begin a new chapter without closing an old one.

We often waste energy worrying about things we cannot change. Instead of learning from the past and moving forward, we stay stuck in old patterns. But rather than focusing on what is beyond your control, shift your attention to what you *can* influence. If something in your life is not working, change it. And if you cannot change it, adjust the way you think about it. The more tightly you cling to expectations of how things "should" be the more disappointment you will encounter. Be the change you wish to see in the world.

To break away from limitations, you must also believe in yourself. Discouragement and failure are often the very stepping stones that lead to success. When you choose hope, you open the door to possibility. Challenges give life meaning; without embracing them, you may never learn how to navigate the storms that prepare you for greater strength. Remember: in every difficulty lies an opportunity, and what appears to be defeat may simply be a signal to press forward. I say this because I have failed many times, yet those failures became the pathway to my victories through the grace of God. So, failure is not the end; it is often just a bend.

Another major obstacle to breaking limitations is distraction. It is one of the enemy's most effective weapons. Jesus tells us in *John 10:10* that 'the thief comes to *steal, kill, and destroy*'. If the enemy cannot destroy your walk with God, he will attempt to steal your focus, especially as you approach breakthroughs. As the saying goes, *what the enemy cannot destroy, he distracts*.

Distraction comes in many forms and from many directions, but the outcome is often the same. It prevents us from embracing new opportunities or steers us off course entirely. It can distort your identity, rush you ahead of God's timing, slow you down, or give you false confidence. Scripture warns in *1 Corinthians 7:35* that we must serve the Lord without distraction, because losing focus on what truly matters weakens our interest and commitment to God's purposes.

Not all distractions are harmful, however. Some can be therapeutic, allowing the mind to temporarily shift away from pain or stress. While the hurt may still exist, redirecting your focus can strengthen your resilience and prepare you to face new challenges.

Still, spiritual distraction is something every believer must continually confront. Even as I counsel others through it, I often discover that I, too, must fight the same battle. Overcoming distraction requires self-awareness and discipline. You must identify the source of your dissatisfaction, confront your distractions, embrace your vision, and take decisive steps toward fulfilling it. Do not allow anyone or anything to divert you from God's assignment for your life.

This book includes contributions from several authors, each writing sincerely and from the heart.

Here are a few guiding principles to help you navigate the hurdles of life:

- Stop feeling sorry for yourself. Instead of sinking into self-pity, take time to reflect and identify where things may have gone wrong and what lessons can be learned.
- Learn to embrace pain, even when it feels unbearable. Some situations cannot be avoided or bypassed. Amidst all, do not lose your focus on Christ.
- When circumstances feel blurry or overwhelming, pray. Prayer still works. It brings clarity, comfort, and hope. *Philippians 4:6-7* reminds us: *"Do not be anxious about anything, but in every situation, by prayer and petition, with thanksgiving, present your requests to God. And the peace of God, which transcends all understanding, will guard your hearts and your minds in Christ Jesus."*
- Even when it appears that prayer has not produced the result you expect, prayer remains the anchor many turn to in times of deep pain. And remember, you cannot become a cornerstone unless you have first been a rejected stone.

A NEW BEGINNING

Prof. Okikijesu

What is a new beginning? It is an opportunity to wipe the slate clean and start afresh. It marks the moment when you step out of one season of life and into another, often at a more advanced, more enlightened level. A new beginning can also be a period of transition, a bridge between what was and what is yet to come.

Throughout the Scripture, new beginnings are often God-ordained moments that grant individuals the chance to start again. From Genesis to Revelation, the Bible is full of real people with real struggles. Their stories teach us powerful lessons about how to respond when God opens the door to a fresh start.

Have you ever wondered how the month of January got its name? January is widely associated with new beginnings because it marks the start of the new year on the Gregorian calendar. Yet no beginning, no matter how symbolic, can flourish without a strong foundation.

Every person is a builder, and every life is a house. The strength of that house depends entirely on its foundation. Just as a builder must follow the blueprint when constructing a physical structure, we must also follow divine instructions when building our lives. There are essential dos and don'ts in this process, but many people choose to ignore or alter the directions. Building a life is much like assembling a DIY product. Leave out one critical piece and patch it together carelessly, and sooner or later, it will collapse.

This is why a true new beginning cannot stand on a faulty foundation. A fresh start must be anchored in truth, wisdom, and obedience if it is to endure.

HOPE

Pastor Esther Aramide Olujimi

Some years ago, I had a complicated pregnancy that challenged my faith. Here I was staring at a baby that had tubes attached to her, while I was also too weak to hold this delicate little one, whom I named Hope.

To address this topic, it is imperative to understand what hope is. Hope can simply be described as a strong expectation in something or someone. Hope and faith are most often referred to as the same thing, and they are indeed very synonymous, but in this discourse, I want to highlight the pillars of hope, the necessity of hope, and the outcome of hope.

Hope is often underrated, regarded as wishful thinking, but the Bible is not silent about the importance of hope in relation to man and God and vice versa. In the scriptural passage *of Acts 28:5,* "And he shook off the beast into the fire and felt no harm," we see faith in action as Paul shook the beast off his hand. Faith was activated when he shook the beast off, but hope came into force when he felt no harm. The belief of those around him was that Paul would suffer from the effects of the beast. Their faith in that mishap was based on what they saw had happened to him, but the hope of Paul negated their expectations. The people around him were responding to what they had seen and heard, but Paul had to step into the dimension of hope to rise above the situation. In the end, they had to change their mind and opinion concerning Paul and instead recorded him as a god.

In Romans 15:13, the Bible says, "May the God of hope fill you with all joy and peace in believing so that by the power of the Holy Spirit, you may abound in hope." This verse reveals two dimensions of hope. Firstly, hope as a character or attribute of God, and secondly, hope as a mechanism of faith through the Holy Spirit. Therefore, the first pillar of hope is God. This attribute of hope is given to every human being; the ability to hope as a feature of our identity with God. It is interesting that nowhere in the scripture is God referred to as "God of Faith" but rather "God of hope," which means that hope is a divine innate ability to trust. Faith has often been referred to as an active belief with corresponding actions, but hope runs deeper. Hope is a revealer of our level of intimacy with God and the challenges that one has faced. The testimony of our struggles and the strength with which we hold our posture in God.

The second pillar of hope is the Holy Spirit. In the book of *Romans 5:13*, we can see that hope can only be sustained by the Holy Spirit. Faith comes in measure from God, as stated in Romans 12:3, "as God hath dealt to every man the measure of faith" through his word. Faith is a byproduct of the seed of the word sown into the heart of man. On the other hand, hope is not necessarily activated by the hearing of the word, but by a relationship with the Father through HIS SPIRIT.

It is possible for faith to meet something that seems bigger than itself, just like the disciples could not heal the child in Matthew 17:16. They had been part of Jesus' miracles, but when they were alone, their faith could not solve the issue. That is the reality of many Christians who hear a great sermon, witness a great testimony, but when the door closes, and they're alone, their faith crumbles. You can have a corresponding action to faith, but it must anchor on hope, which focuses on God rather than on the action of faith.

We see this clearly in the story of Peter when he walked on water towards Jesus. His faith made him get out of the boat, but by focusing on the action of walking on the water, he lost sight of Jesus and started to drown; he was doing the right thing as commanded by Jesus, but his attention was on the wrong thing. A lot of believers so engrossed in faith actions that they lose sight of the person and presence of God in their situation. This story in the book of Matthew 14:22-33 Is a reminder that faith without hope does not have proper ground. Our hope ensures that as we carry out faith actions prompted by the Holy Spirit, we are looking past the situation to see our creator in his glory.

The third pillar is God's glory. In the book of Romans 5:1-5, the apostle Paul, in verse 2, talks about our access into the grace of justification and relationship with God through Christ, which enabled the father-child relationship. This access allows us to behold the glory of the Father through Christ (John 1:14). Moses prayed to see the glory of God in *Exodus 33:18,* a privilege reserved until *Matthew 17.* Why was Moses so vested in this glory? Because His glory reveals His person and His power. That's why we can rejoice in hope of our anticipation to see and know HIM. Every revelation from the Holy Spirit is to give us a glimpse of His glory.

Moreover, hope comes alive as we walk through the corridors of challenges. In *Romans 5,* hope is a process that starts with tribulations; the trying of our faith that births patience. After we develop patience, we move to the level of experience, spiritual maturity, which then leads to hope. Without these main components, hope can seem like a fairy tale.

Lastly, there is no shame in hope. In Romans 4:18, the bible says Abraham believed in hope even when the odds were stacked against him, because he believed in the power of God to make the promise happen. God is sold out to our hope in Him, and we can lean on His love to see us through. The love of God was more evident in my life when I walked out of the hospital, leaving my baby in the hospital. How could I possibly go home not knowing if I would come back to see her the following day? My eyes would fill with tears every day I had to leave her. But the God of hope remained faithful even when my faith failed.

FAITH

Pastor Babatunde Soniregun

What Is Faith?

Faith is believing that the promises of God are true. It is trusting and hoping in God, putting all weight upon Him, yielding all to Him alone, and reclining in the everlasting arms of God.

Faith removes doubts and banishes burdens. It produces perfect peace amid alarms. Faith, when joined with hope, becomes a route for life's journey, leading the believer to the divine assignment of God.

Why Faith Is Important

Faith is a spiritual force that produces living proof because Jesus is the living Word of God. *John 6:63* states: "The words that I speak to you are spirit, and they are life."

Faith is rooted in the living Word of God. *Romans 10:17* declares: "So, then faith comes by hearing, and hearing by the word of God."

Faith is not philosophy or ideology; it is a spiritual force. To be faithful is to possess a key for dominion on the face of the earth. Jesus said: "If you can believe, all things are possible to him who believes." *(Mark 9:23).*

Faith as a Living Spiritual Force

Faith is a living spiritual force that provokes God to respond. It was faith that caused God to deliver the three friends of Daniel from the burning fiery furnace of King Nebuchadnezzar (*Daniel 3).*

Hebrews 11:1 defines faith as: "The substance of things hoped for, the evidence of things not seen." Faith must move beyond talk-faith. True faith taps into the power of God through hearing and hearing His Word.

Faith Released Through Hearing

Mark 5:25–29 records the account of a woman who had a flow of blood for twelve years. She suffered many things from many physicians and spent all she had, yet grew worse.

When she heard about Jesus, she came behind Him in the crowd and touched His garment, saying: "If only I may touch His clothes, I shall be made well."

Immediately, she was healed.

Certainly—here is a faith-centered completion that flows naturally from your passage and keeps a reverent, biblical tone:

Though a great multitude thronged Jesus, her faith enabled her to touch and draw power from Him. Jesus responded, "Who touched My clothes?" (*Mark 5:30*). Faith distinguishes a believing touch from a surrounding crowd.

While many pressed against Him, only one reached Him in faith. That touch was not accidental; it was intentional, born from hearing, believing, and acting upon the Word. In that moment, faith became the channel through which divine power flowed.

The woman came trembling, knowing what had taken place within her. Jesus turned to her, not to rebuke her, but to reveal the principle of faith. He declared, "Daughter, your faith has made you well. Go in peace and be healed of your affliction." (*Mark 5:34*).

Her healing was not merely the result of physical contact, but of faith that trusted completely in Christ. Faith drew virtue where the crowd drew nothing. Faith-activated power where mere proximity produced no change.

In the same way, faith still distinguishes today. It is not how close one stands to Jesus, but how fully one believes and commits to Him. Faith reaches beyond the crowd, touches the living Word, and releases the power of God.

Faith as a Spiritual Weapon

Faith is a spiritual force and an important weapon that keeps the devil and his agents at bay, giving life to the living Word of God. *Ephesians 6:16* declares: “Above all, taking the shield of faith with which you will be able to quench all the fiery darts of the wicked one.”

Continual hearing of the Word of God strengthens faith as a shield against the enemies of this wicked world. Faith Is Commitment to His command. It is a commitment to God’s commanding Word.

Such commitment is necessary to break through where there seems to be no way. Faith comes from the living Word of God, not from the world.

Conclusion

Faith is a spiritual force that believes, hears, commits, and acts. It is anchored in God's Word and releases divine power when exercised. Through faith, believers overcome, walk in dominion, and fulfil God's divine assignment for their lives.

If you are reading this book and going through a rough time, please hold on to this truth: your season does not define your destination.

Faith reminds us that even when the road is hard, God is still in control. What feels like a setback can be a setup for growth, strength, and deeper trust in Him.

Do not let fear or discouragement speak louder than faith. The Word of God assures us that He is close to the broken-hearted and that He gives strength to those who feel weak.

Even when you cannot see a way forward, trust that God is making one. Faith often works quietly, behind the scenes, long before the breakthrough appears.

Take each day one step at a time. Speak hope over your situation, even when emotions say otherwise. Faith is not about denying the pain; it is believing that pain is not the end of the story. What you are facing today will not last forever, but the strength you gain from it will.

Remember, you are not forgotten, and you are not alone. God's promises are still true in the storm. Keep believing, keep praying, and keep moving forward. What you are walking through now can become a testimony of faith, resilience, and victory in time. "This is coming from someone who has been through the mill and is still standing. It is well with you.

ACCOMPLISHMENT

Apostle Samuel Terry

WHAT IS THE BIBLICAL MEANING OF ACCOMPLISHMENT?

Accomplishment, in a biblical sense, is the fulfilment of God's will through faithful obedience, perseverance, and trust in Him. Scripture teaches that true accomplishment is not defined by human applause, wealth, or power, but by alignment with God's purpose. From the beginning, God entrusted humanity with responsibility, calling Adam to tend the garden and steward creation. This reveals that accomplishment begins with obedience to divine instruction and care for what God places in our hands.

Throughout the Bible, men and women accomplished great works not by their own strength, but by faith. Noah accomplished God's command by building the ark despite ridicule, proving that obedience outweighs public opinion.

Abraham's accomplishment was counted to him as righteousness because he believed God's promise, even when fulfilment seemed impossible. Moses accomplished his calling not by eloquence but by reliance on God's power to deliver His people.

Jesus Christ provides the ultimate picture of accomplishment. He declared, "It is finished," not because the journey was easy, but because He completed the work the Father gave Him. His accomplishment was rooted in love, sacrifice, and submission to God's will. Through Him, believers learn that accomplishment often requires endurance, humility, and surrender.

Biblically, accomplishment is measured by faithfulness rather than results. The Apostle Paul reminds us that one may plant, and another may water, but God gives the increase. Therefore, accomplishment is not about controlling outcomes, but about committing to obedience. When a believer walks faithfully in God's calling, every act done in love and obedience becomes a lasting accomplishment in the sight of God.

CONCLUSION

When you are going through a difficult season and feel far from accomplishing what you hoped for, remember that hardship does not cancel purpose. In the Bible, many people experienced long periods of waiting, struggle, and seeming failure before their work bore fruit. Delay is not denial, and struggle is not proof that you are failing.

It is important to understand that accomplishment is not always visible right away. Sometimes, the greatest growth happens quietly—in patience, character, and faith. Scripture reminds us not to grow weary in doing good, for in due season we will reap if we do not give up. Tough times often refine us, preparing us for what lies ahead.

Be gentle with yourself. Accomplishment is not measured by comparison with others or by meeting every expectation at once. Take small, faithful steps and trust that God sees your effort, even when results are unclear. Pray for wisdom and strength. Allow yourself to rest when needed. Rest is not quitting; it is part of endurance.

Finally, remember that your worth is not tied to what you produce. You are valuable because you were created with purpose. Even in hardship, God is at work, shaping your path. Stay faithful, remain hopeful, and trust that this season, though difficult, can become part of a greater accomplishment in your life.

My accomplishment today, to the glory of God, is proof that failure is never final. It is proof that with determination, patience, and belief, we can rise above challenges and build something lasting. And if by God's grace, I can write about this after so many failures and slippery ladders, so can you. Let your struggles become the foundation of your accomplishment, because every scar tells the story of your strength."

God can turn any situation into a testimony of His faithfulness. Our perseverance and resilience may have led to success despite past failures, but sometimes, we may not have noticed.

Believers, like Paul, are called to walk in faith, knowing that their lives are tools for God to change hearts and reveal His glory. We all can as well. Be blessed.

WHAT IS ENDURANCE?

Prophetess Mercy Magbagbeola

Biblical endurance is the spiritual strength to remain faithful, obedient, and hopeful under pressure, suffering, or delay, amidst all, trusting God even when circumstances are painful or unclear.

In Scripture, endurance is not passive resignation. It is an active and steadfast faith.

Endurance

Endurance is the God-given ability to remain faithful, obedient, and steadfast through prolonged trials without surrendering trust in God. It is not passive waiting, but active perseverance, continuing to believe, obey, and hope even when the journey is hard.

Throughout the Scripture, endurance is revealed through the lives of men and women who remained faithful under pressure and saw God's power revealed in due time.

Endurance in the Life of Job

Job's life is a powerful testimony of endurance. Though he lost his possessions, his children, and his health, Job refused to abandon his faith in God. In the midst of intense suffering, he declared:

"Though He slay me, yet will I trust Him." (*Job 13:15*)

Job endured misunderstanding, pain, and silence, yet remained faithful. In the end, God restored him and blessed his latter days more than his beginning (*Job 42:10–12*). His story reveals that endurance preserves faith until restoration comes.

Endurance in Joseph's Journey

Joseph endured betrayal by his brothers, slavery, false accusation, and imprisonment. For years, the promise God gave him seemed forgotten. Yet Joseph remained faithful in every season.

Scripture records that "the Lord was with Joseph" even in prison (*Genesis 39:21*). His endurance positioned him for elevation, and in God's time, Joseph rose to become ruler in Egypt, declaring:

"You meant evil against me, but God meant it for good." (*Genesis 50:20*) Endurance transforms suffering into purpose.

Endurance in the Life of David

David endured years of persecution while waiting for God's promise of kingship. Though anointed as king, he fled from Saul, living in caves and wilderness places. Yet David refused to take matters into his own hands. He trusted God's timing, saying: "Wait on the Lord; be of good courage, and He shall strengthen your heart." (*Psalm 27:14*)

David's endurance preserved his integrity and prepared him for leadership.

Endurance in the Ministry of Jesus Christ

Jesus demonstrated the ultimate endurance. He endured rejection, betrayal, suffering, and the cross for the joy set before Him. *Hebrews 12:2* declares: "Who for the joy that was set before Him endured the cross, despising the shame."

Through endurance, salvation was made available to all mankind. His life teaches that endurance is often the pathway to victory and glory.

Endurance in the Early Church

The apostles endured persecution, imprisonment, and hardship for the sake of the Gospel. Paul testified: "We are hard-pressed on every side yet not crushed; we are perplexed, but not in despair." *(2 Corinthians 4:8)* Their endurance strengthened the Church and advanced the kingdom of God.

Biblical endurance is sustained by faith, hope, and trust in God. It does not deny hardship but refuses to surrender to it. Endurance holds on until God's purpose is fulfilled.

As Scripture reminds us: "He who endures to the end shall be saved." (*Matthew 24:13*) Endurance is the bridge between God's promise and its fulfilment.

Conclusion

Endurance is the quiet faith that keeps going when quitting feels reasonable.

God honours endurance not because it is easy, but because it reflects but because it reflects courage, perseverance, and deep faith in the midst of trials.

Many stories in the Bible have taught me so much about endurance in my everyday life. I am happy to share one with our readers.

The Lamp That Would Not Go Out

In a small village near the hills of Judah, there lived an old man named Eliab who served as the keeper of the temple lamps. Every evening, as the sun sank low, he would light the lamps and tend them through the night.

One year, a great famine came upon the land. Oil became scarce, and many lamps in the village went dark. Friends urged Eliab to stop. "Why waste the little oil you have?" they asked. "God understands." But Eliab remembered the words of the Lord: "The light of the righteous shall not be put out." So, each night, though his hands trembled and his supply seemed too small, he lit the lamp and prayed. Some nights, the oil looked barely enough. Yet morning after morning, the lamp still burned.

One evening, a weary traveller saw the light and followed it to the temple. There, he found hope, rest, and faith restored. Soon, others came. The lamp became a sign that God had not abandoned His people. When the famine ended, Eliab looked into the jar and found it not empty, but still holding oil.

And the Lord whispered to his heart: "You endured when you could not see the end. My strength was hidden in your faithfulness."

"Let us not grow weary in doing good, for in due season we shall reap, if we do not lose heart." Galatians 6:9.

The power of Endurance is more than just a skill. It is a mindset. It represents the power to face difficult circumstances, the persistence to continue when everything seems to be against you, and the resilience to rise after every fall. By training our bodies, our hearts, and our spirits, we can cultivate an enduring spirit that helps us to overcome challenges and grow stronger in the process.

Endurance teaches us that the journey is just as important as the destination. It is through enduring hardships that we unlock our full potential and learn the true extent of our strength. God bless you all.

MERCY

Evangelist Rabbi Joel Adegoke

What is Mercy?

Being a word affiliated with God (Divine), we must go into His word (Holy Bible) for an accurate definition. The first place this word was mentioned was in Genesis chapter nineteen, verse nineteen, (KJV).

Do you think that was a coincidence? And the last place this word was mentioned is in Jude chapter one, verse twenty-one. *Genesis 19:19* Behold now, thy servant hath found grace in thy sight, and thou hast magnified thy mercy, which thou hast shewed unto me in saving my life; and I cannot escape to the mountain, lest some evil take me, and I die:

Jude 1:21 Keep yourselves in the love of God, looking for the mercy of our Lord Jesus Christ unto eternal life. The same word mercy in Hebrew is Hanan; in Yoruba is Anu, meaning to be gracious (in verb). But (in noun) it means pity; compassion; clemency. All these descriptions are aiming at survival and Hope.

Therefore, mercy can be defined as the grace of God that led us to eternal life. *Romans 5:18* says: Therefore, as by the offence of one judgment came upon all men to condemnation: even so by the righteousness of one the free gift came upon all men unto justification of life.19 For as by one man's disobedience many were made sinners, so by the obedience of one shall many be made righteous. 20. Moreover, the law entered that the offence might abound. But where sin abounded, grace did much more abound: 21. That as sin hath reigned unto death, even so might grace reign through righteousness unto eternal life by Jesus Christ our Lord. Mercy is the power or nature of God that led us back to Him. Mercy remained a gift as it cannot be acquired by human effort, which is affiliated and sometimes called favour. Who is grace, who is Jesus Christ that was given to human beings, now believers, to bring them back into Jesus Christ, which is eternal life -John 1:4 In him was life; and the life was the light of men.

Why the need for Mercy?

The initial creation was based on mercy, and everything created was kept in mercy according to John 1:1-6, and in a lot of places in the scripture from Genesis to Revelation, it is all about mercy. However, we disengaged from the mercy and were sent away in mercy, because without mercy, we cannot operate in any form or shape.

Acts 17:28 For in him we live, and move, and have our being; as certain also of your own poets have said, for we are also his offspring. Therefore, since the time of Adam and Eve, mercy has been speaking, active, and leading us back to Himself. Mercy spoke to Cain and was rejected. Not until Seth gave birth to his son Enosh did people start calling upon the name of the Lord in mercy that they may be saved.

People who believe in mercy continue to seek Him, and those who did not reject Him. Because Adam received mercy, Abel received mercy, Enoch received mercy, and Noah received mercy, Abram received mercy, Rahab received mercy, and so on, until it comes to our era, mercy appeared in the form of man, according to the prediction of God through the prophets. Isaiah 7:14 Therefore, the Lord himself shall give you a sign; Behold, a virgin shall conceive, and bear a son, and shall call his name Immanuel. 15. Butter and honey shall he eat, that he may know to refuse the evil, and choose the good.16 For before the child

shall know to refuse the evil, and choose the good, the land that thou abhorrest shall be forsaken of both her kings. The sign is the son, and the son is the mercy of God to humanity for those who believe and are called according to His purpose, just like Abel and Cain, David and Saul, Ephraim and Manasseh, Ruth and Orpah, Moses and Pharaoh, etc. Because it is something beyond our capability, we rely on His gifting of the same. Hence, He declared that I will have mercy on whoever I will have mercy (Paraphrase) Exodus 33:19 And he said, I will make all my goodness pass before thee, and I will proclaim the name of the Lord before thee; and will be gracious to whom I will be gracious, and will shew mercy on whom I will shew mercy. Rom 9:15 For he saith to Moses, I will have mercy on whom I will have mercy, and I will have compassion on whom I will have compassion.

The mercy from man is expectant, but the mercy of God is free gain. No one can take us back to our position apart from God, for you are saved through faith, not of your works (paraphrase).

We bless the name of God for His mercy, grace, compassion, kindness, and love. We have come to know His attributes.

LIVING IN THE REALMS OF POSSIBILITIES

Pastor Honey Emmanuel-Molokwu

As this journey through the Scroll of Possibilities comes to a close, one truth stands unshaken: life is never void of possibilities when hope is alive and faith is active. Every page you have encountered was written to remind you that no season, however dark, delayed, or demanding, has the final word.

Hope teaches us to see beyond what is, into what can be. Faith gives us the courage to trust God even when the path is unclear. Endurance strengthens us to remain standing when answers seem slow in coming. Mercy reminds us that we are sustained not by perfection, but by grace, both received and extended. Perseverance keeps us moving forward when quitting feels easier than continuing.

Together, these virtues form the foundation of a life anchored in divine possibility. They assure us that setbacks are not endings, waiting seasons are not wasted, and failures are not fatal. What appears impossible in human sight becomes possible in God's timing and purpose.

This book is not merely meant to be read; it is meant to be lived. Let its message guide your choices, shape your responses, and strengthen your resolve. Carry hope into uncertain moments. Walk by faith when logic fails. Endure trials with quiet confidence. Show mercy generously. Persevere relentlessly.

As you close this book, may you open a new chapter in your life, one filled with courage, expectation, and unwavering trust in God. The possibilities before you are limitless, and your story is far from finished.

The 'Scroll of Possibilities' does not end here; it begins in you.

A special thanks to Dr Prophetess Deborah OkikiJesu for the privilege of contributing to this book. I salute your dedication and selfless service to God's kingdom.

ABOUT THE AUTHOR

Prof. Deborah Titilayo Okikijesu is a Minister, Professional, and Humanitarian.

Revd Deborah Titilayo Okiki Jesu is a distinguished licensed Minister of God whose impactful spiritual work is mirrored by her professional commitment to the Health and Social Care Services. She brings a wealth of knowledge and expertise to every sphere of her influence, holding multiple academic degrees from various reputable institutions both in the UK and internationally.

Her roles extend far beyond the professional and ministerial, reflecting a deep dedication to serving others. She is a revered mother and grandmother. A compassionate counsellor, an inspiring motivational speaker, and a prolific author. Her commitment to humanity is further demonstrated through her extensive humanitarian work.

The foundation of her mandate rests on a profound, non-denominational calling. Driven by the grace of God's anointing. Her ministry transcends racial and cultural boundaries, enabling her to impact people of all backgrounds positively. She is dedicated solely to fulfilling her divine mission, regardless of religious affiliation.

By the special grace of God, she is the visionary founder of the El Bethel Prayer Tabernacle Worldwide, a ministry currently headquartered in London, UK, which continues to grow as a centre for prayer, counsel, and global outreach.